ideals® AUTUMN

'Tis pleasant on a fine spring morn
To see the buds expand;
'Tis pleasant in the summertime
To see the fruitful land;
'Tis pleasant on a winter's night
To sit around the blaze;
But what are joys like these, my boys,
To merry autumn days!

We hail the merry autumn days
When leaves are turning red,
Because they're far more beautiful
Than anyone has said.
We hail the merry harvesttime,
The gayest of the year,
The time of rich and bounteous crops,
Rejoicing and good cheer.

Charles Dickens

ISBN 0-8249-1045-1

Publisher, Patricia A. Pingry
Editor, Ramona Richards
Art Director, David Lenz
Permissions, Kathleen Gilbert
Copy Editor, Peggy Schaefer
Phototypesetter, Tammy Walsh

IDEALS—Vol. 43, No. 6 September MCMLXXXVI IDEALS (ISSN 0019-137X) is published eight times a year,
February, March, May, June, August, September, November, December
by IDEALS PUBLISHING CORPORATION, Nelson Place at Elm Hill Pike, Nashville, Tenn. 37214-8000
Second class postage paid at Nashville, Tennessee, and additional mailing offices.
Copyright © MCMLXXXVI by IDEALS PUBLISHING CORPORATION.
POSTMASTER: Send address changes to Ideals, Post Office Box 148000, Nashville, Tenn. 37214-8000
All rights reserved. Title IDEALS registered U.S. Patent Office.
Published simultaneously in Canada.

SINGLE ISSUE—$3.50
ONE-YEAR SUBSCRIPTION—eight consecutive issues as published—$15.95
TWO-YEAR SUBSCRIPTION—sixteen consecutive issues as published—$27.95
Outside U.S.A., add $4.00 per subscription year for postage and handling.

Front and back covers by Fred Sieb

Inside front cover by Ed Cooper

Inside back cover from Cyr Color Photo

October

This month the trees begin to make
Their autumn alterations;
October brings the turning leaf
In flaming variations!

Triumphant beauty clothes the hills;
The mountains are ablaze!
There's splendor everywhere to see
These gold autumnal days!

Then one day soon the whistling winds
Will hustle-bustle by,
Sending leaves a-sprawling with
A wistful, wind-swept sigh!

This month the trees begin to make
Their autumn alterations;
October brings the blowing leaf
In flaming variations!

Georgia B. Adams

Photo Opposite
WAGON WHEEL
Dick Smith

Autumn Leavings

When the strains of "September Song" and "Autumn Leaves" begin to be played on the radio each year, I know it is time to begin my annual autumn leavings.

It's time to shake the sand out of the rugs and blankets, to fetch the last special shell from behind the bookcase and cast it back upon the beach. Summer fuscias and chartreuses need to be folded and tucked away, straw hats shelved, sandals stacked. Beach towels and barbeques must be put to rest from all their busy labors.

Summer is such a garish, self-important season, proudly parading under a blaring yellow sun and impossibly blue sky. Summer shouts all day and hums all night—never still, never silent—always yelling at me to come outside to play. I won't be sorry to say good-bye to summer for awhile.

Autumn's golds and crimsons ignite the hills in quiet fire and bid me leave behind the summer's heat. Say farewell to icy lemonade and minty teas, and welcome cider steeped in handmade mugs as earthy as the season. Cinnamon and clove overcome the lighter scents of summer as we gather 'round the crackling fire again. We leave the days of summer when we were scattered by vacations and cling to hearth and home once more.

The hummingbird and lark are quiet, but in the crisping air the urgent call of southbound geese is heard. In the fog-swept dawns and hazy afternoons, their jagged arrow points to distant nests. They take their autumn leavings, too, glad for the changing cycles of their lives.

Sky and field abound with autumn's wealth. The harvest moon reflects the golden pumpkins ripening in the patch, as if it waits to be some night-child's jack-o-lantern. Corn stalks stand like awkward sentinels guarding the rich, dark loam beneath their feet. Apples, bursting with sweet juice, hang heavy on the trees. I shall not be sad to leave summer's tender melons for the autumn orchard's crispy bounty.

I leave, not too reluctantly, the spontaneous dance that summer pipes, and turn again to the more ordered, businesslike march of fall. Crisp mornings beckon me to bustle out of bed, get organized, accomplish things. Early twilights urge reflection upon a day's work well done.

Oh, let the melancholy poets paint a dismal picture of summer's end and fall's advent. Let musicians play in minor keys. But when the first leaf falls and smoke-scents hover in the gold of late afternoon, I shall gladly contemplate my autumn leavings.

Pamela Kennedy

September Morn

Oh, happy bright September morn,
  how sweet and soft you are,
How very warm your morning sun,
  how bright your evening star.
Across the hilltops dawning breaks,
  to start a full new day.
The world is fair and nature smiles,
  as autumn finds her way.

Oh, red and gold September morn,
  with clear skies overhead
As summer slowly bids farewell, and
  autumn smiles instead,
How gentle is the sighing breeze as
  treetops turn to gold,
And somewhere in the distance clear,
  an autumn story's told.

Oh, kissed with dew September morn,
  you've brought my heart a thrill.
Your laughter rings in sweet delight,
  on every golden hill.
The roses bloom in softest hues,
  though leaves are tumbling down.
There's gorgeous beauty unsur-
  passed, in country and in town.

Oh, precious dear September morn,
  so melancholy now
The green has changed to red and
  gold on every windswept bough.
Old Mother Nature reaches forth to
  glorify her earth.
Oh, heavenly September morn, how
  can we judge your worth?

Garnett Ann Schultz

Photo Opposite
MT. AND LAKE CHOCURUA, NH
Fred Sieb

Days of Indian Summer

Those last few weeks of summer,
When the sun's a golden glow,
Bring a newness barely noticeable;
Yet, it's in the air . . . I know.

Some call it just the summer's end
Or the first faint sign of fall,
But I prefer it called Indian summer,
The very best time of all.

The days have lost their scorching heat;
The nights are breezy and warm.
The earth's content and close to God,
Still far from winter's harm.

There's a warmth, a gentle fulfillment
That penetrates and settles the sod
In a blanket of rich contentment
Known only by the hand of God.

I hear the hum of nature's things
That crawl and fly by day,
And listen to crickets chirp at night,
And wonder what they say.

Perhaps they talk of passing time,
Or the winds or the brooks that murmur;
But I'm sure they sense that all is well
In days of Indian summer.

Ilene J. Cornwell

Wild Geese

Out of the vast, unclouded sky they come
   Like homing pigeons to a stable loft.
A mighty convoy slowly coming in,
   Suspended far above . . . they swing aloft,
Then circle slowly waiting to alight,
   Then come in one by one in perfect flight.

The leader of the squadron walks around,
   Ruffles his feathers, preens himself a bit.
He almost seems to count his special flock,
   Assuring himself that all is well with it,
And then he turns, with quite a lordly air,
   To gorge himself upon the bill of fare.

Whence do they come and whither do they go,
   These royal travellers of the quiet sky
By tens and thousands passing over head,
   Leaving to us the memory of a cry,
Full of the lonely trails they travel o'er
   From the warm southland to the Arctic's shore.

And we . . . we watch them winging out of sight,
To wish them Godspeed in their lonely flight.

Edna Jaques

Canoe Country

Mystery lowers its veil of night
Softly, gently on my enchanted sight.
Lapping waters and whispering pines;
A path of silver where the moon reclines.

Echoing calls of the laughing loons;
Black ducks feeding in hidden lagoons.
Here the great blue heron builds his nest,
And islands float on the water's breast.

Haunting memories that capture bliss;
The paddle hands that the sunbeams kiss;
Old tote roads lost in the muskeg sedge;
A campfire gleaming on a granite ledge.

The sudden slap of a beaver's tail;
A lone wolf's howl in the mounting gale;
A speckled trout in a quiet pool;
A northern pike where the whitecaps rule.

A portage around the rapid's roar;
A path worn smooth on the forest floor;
Packs that are heavy yet feathery light;
Yokes that bruise and are forgotten by night.

The northern lights on the weaving loom
And stars displayed in the glory room;
Sunshine and shadow and scent of pine;
Cumulus clouds fringed with gold and wine.

A chain of lakes and rivers and streams
To recall at night in pleasant dreams;
The pipes of Pan to wonder the mind;
Ties of friendship that will forever bind.

Spirits that whisper of Indian lore;
Voyageurs' ghosts on the distant shore;
Melodies played on wind's harpsichord;
Peace and beauty that nature has stored.

A. Z. Nelson

Photo Overleaf
MT. SHUKSAN, WA
George Schwartz

Autumn Color

Jack Frost paints a portrait of beauty
With colors so vivid and bright;
It's framed with a purple misty haze
And draped in a frosty night.

Big, fat, bright orange pumpkins
Nestle snugly among shocks of corn;
Leaves flutter silently earthward;
Ice sparkles like glass in the dawn.

The nuts drop softly upon the ground,
Leaves fall and hide them there;
Squirrels work away industriously,
Their winter store to prepare.

A pale harvest moon sails serenely
Across a star-studded sky,
And smiles on a world full of color
Since Jack Frost has just passed by.

Mrs. Paul E. King

In Those Work Together Days

Oh, there lingers in my memory,
And I fondly recall,
The thrashing in the summer
And the husking in the fall,
When the neighbors got together
As we went from farm to farm.
And the way we joined in labor
Kind of leaves a special charm.

Oh, those working days together
Seemed to draw us into one;
We depended on each other
Till the harvest days were done.
Now so many things are different
As we farm our several ways;
Yet, I kind of have a longing
For those "work-together" days.

Daniel D. Rodes

Hearty Harvest One-Dish Meals

Navarin of Lamb
Makes 4 servings

2 pounds lamb shoulder, cut in 1½-inch cubes
  Salt and freshly ground pepper
1 tablespoon vegetable oil
4 cups chicken broth
1 to 2 cloves garlic, minced or pressed
1 bay leaf, broken in half
¼ teaspoon thyme *or* rosemary leaves
2 large tomatoes, seeded and chopped

4 new potatoes, quartered
4 turnips, peeled, and cut in 1½-inch pieces
4 carrots, peeled and cut in 1½-inch pieces
1 10-ounce package frozen pearl onions
1 10-ounce package frozen early peas, thawed

Season lamb with salt and pepper to taste. Heat oil in a large saucepan or Dutch oven. Brown lamb on all sides. Remove lamb from pan; pat dry with paper towels. Wipe pan clean. Return meat to pan. Add broth, garlic, bay leaves, thyme, and tomatoes. Bring to a boil; reduce heat. Simmer for 45 minutes then add potatoes, turnips, and carrots. Simmer for 20 minutes. Add onions; simmer for 15 minutes. Add peas; simmer for 5 minutes or until lamb is tender. Remove meat and vegetables from pan. Skim fat from the cooking liquid. Return lamb to pan. Gently stir lamb and vegetables together. Adjust seasonings, if needed. Heat and serve.

One-Pot Goulash
Makes 8 servings

2 pounds beef round, fat trimmed, cut in cubes
1 tablespoon vegetable oil
1½ cups water
2 red onions, chopped
½ teaspoon salt
¼ teaspoon freshly ground pepper

1 tablespoon paprika
½ teaspoon caraway seeds
1 8-ounce can tomatoes
1 8-ounce can tomato purée
8 ounces fusili noodles, multi-colored and fresh, if possible

Brown meat in oil in a heavy Dutch oven or pressure cooker. Add water; bring to a boil. Drain off water into separate container; set aside until fat rises to surface. Skim off fat with a bulb-type baster; return liquid to pot. Stir in all remaining ingredients except noodles. Cover and simmer over very low heat for 1 hour or until tender, or cook in a pressure cooker for 20 minutes, following manufacturer's directions. Stir in noodles. Add more water, if needed. Cover and cook an additional 10 to 12 minutes (or 5 minutes under pressure).

Country Crocks

When we visited my grandmother's house in the country, the most mysterious or intriguing place of all on the farm was the cool, dark, damp cellar. After harvesttime, this was the place to be. Great pyramids of apples and potatoes filled the bins, and the shelves in the fruit cellar were loaded to capacity with two-quart, quart, and pint jars of fruits, vegetables, preserves, pickles, jellies, and meats. Grandma's cellar was filled with the pleasing scent of fresh apples, potatoes, turnips, and other delectable root vegetables. Nestled up in corners of all the huge cellars underneath the farmhouse were country crocks of all sizes which were filled with preserved foods for the long, hard winter that was always expected. These were the days when there were no refrigerators or freezers to preserve food, and the cellar bottom was the place to store the round, beige, earthenware crocks with the dark brown necks. How fascinating it was to have Grandma lift the plate and rock weighing it down off the top of the huge crock of sauerkraut. It was truly delicious served for dinner with pork roast or hot dogs.

When Grandma wanted something for supper, she seldom made a trip to the store; her supplies were in the cellar. Her country crocks contained delicious dill pickles, meats in brine, apple butter, and eggs preserved in brine and red wines. Aged cheese and butter were also stored in small crocks. There was always a plate to cover the smaller crocks, topped with a heavy rock or stone to discourage a hungry country mouse; and the larger crocks were covered with tin covers, topped with rocks to weigh them down.

Some of the crocks were used to store applesauce, candied cherries, pickled pears, relishes, or mincemeats for short lengths of time; and the cool cellar was just the place to set a crock of jello. I wouldn't want to be without today's refrigerators and freezers, but believe we can unlatch the magic of the country crocks in this day and age.

Country crocks are once again on the scene with mouth-watering cheeses, butter, pickles, preserves, and jellies being put up in this manner. The country crocks have been around all this time, and the blending of the country crocks of yesteryear with modern day living gives moments of joyful pleasure to those with nostalgic memories of the past.

Helen M. Oakley

A Trust in Others

Along a winding country road
Where hues of autumn glow,
There stands a cart-shaped roadside stand
With produce row on row.

Amidst this produce stands a jar,
The printing on it says:
"Please help yourself; put money here;
We trust you and God bless."

Along this scenic country road
These harvest gifts are placed,
Together with man's trust in man,
A trust time cannot change.

Loise Pinkerton Fritz

The County Fair

The county fair is a bright balloon
Carried on a string,
An ice cream cone and popcorn stand,
A many-splendored thing.

The county fair is a hundred things
All to see and do . . .
A daring act, a flower show.
It's cotton candy, too.

The county fair is a gay midway,
A cupid for a prize . . .
A shooting match, a thrilling ride
For every age and size.

The county fair is blue ribbon day
For every canning mom
Whose jar is judged the best of all . . .
Such gay ones to choose from.

The county fair is the farmer's day
With prize steers in the rings;
The best of crops, the fowls, the pets . . .
The county fair's many things.

Laurie Dawson

BONFIRE

I love to see a bonfire glow
    When dusk is settling on the town,
Making a little zone of light
    Amid the shadows dim and brown.
The embers glow like isinglass
    Against the dull brown of the grass.

Perchance an old man with a rake
    Gathers the dead leaves in a pile,
While children watch the tiny fire,
    Standing around it single file,
Outlined against the purple night
    Like druids at some pagan rite.

The blue smoke reaching to the sky
  Is fragrant as a bride's bouquet.
The breath of sun-dried leaves and grass
  Is like the smell of new-mown hay,
With now and then a piece of bark
  Burning like incense in the dark.

Beneath the fire's lovely light
  Faces take on a softer look,
And little children from our street
  Look like gay pictures in a book.
And I beheld a miracle
  Under the fire's golden spell.

To lift the full and commonplace
Into a realm of love and grace.

Edna Jaques

Autumn's Last Fling

Autumn is behaving in a most
   unseemly way!
She flourishes her soft paint brush,
   defying winter's grey.
She waves a gay farewell
   to robins on the wing,
Then decked in rainbow colors,
   she begins one last long fling.

She ripples waters and swirls
   leaves in syncopated style;
To young and old she seems to say:
   "Let's play a little while!"
The tall pine trees sigh blissfully
   as if they, too, agree:
All outdoors is uniting in this
   autumnal spree!

Lillian Elizabeth Turner

Red Brick Country Schools: Cornerstones of Modern Education

A leisurely drive along country roads reveals the remains of yesterday's educational systems—one room, red brick schoolhouses. They represent the district schools of the late 1800s and early 1900s and are the cornerstones of modern education. They stand in rather substantial numbers as monuments to an earlier age when education meant learning the basics. The buildings bring back memories of reading, writing, and ciphering taught at the recitation bench, tugging on the bell rope, and keeping the fire burning in the potbelly stove on cold winter days.

The clamor of those classrooms has long since been silent, and most of the schoolhouses have been unused since the 1930s. Many stand empty and rotting—continual targets of vandalism. Windowless and full of debris, with the sky showing through the roof where large areas of slate are missing, these old schools are little more than sanctuaries for birds and rodents. Some, however, have escaped this fate. A few have been converted into handsome, comfortable homes, while others serve as antique shops, farm storage buildings, or advertising billboards. A rare few have even been lovingly restored as schoolhouses, complete with desks, chalkboards, potbelly stoves, and recitation benches.

One of these is Newville Township District #3 School in DeKalb County in the northeastern corner of Indiana. It was built in 1897 and was known as "Mudsock School" because of muddy spring conditions. David and Maxine Ford, owners of the school, have turned it into a private museum and on-going hobby. Mrs. Ford, a third grade teacher, treats her class to a day at "Mudsock" every year.

Hancock County (Ohio) Retired Teachers Association members, many of whom began

their education or taught in one-room schools, pooled their talents to revitalize a badly deteriorating school east of Findlay, Ohio. The reborn "Little Red Schoolhouse" has been open for tours since being rededicated in 1973.

In 1975, Bowling Green State University, Bowling Green, Ohio, reconstructed a one-room schoolhouse on its campus. It is now the university's Center for Educational Memorabilia and is visited regularly by elementary school classes.

The voices of children regularly echo through the Aboite Township District #5 School west of Fort Wayne, Indiana. More than 10,000 have had a quick course in the three R's there since it was refurbished in 1973. Former college history teacher, Linda Huge, puts on period teacher garb to give modern students a taste of 1893 education and discipline.

The brick schoolhouses generally had one large room, an alcove on either side of the entrance for coats and lunch boxes, wooden floors, and 13 to 15-foot-high ceilings. Most of the schools have steeply pitched slate roofs, a bell tower, and high, narrow arched windows and doorways. A stone nameplate over the door identifies the township and gives the district number and year the building was completed.

With the exception of the earliest buildings, which were very plain, the most noticeable differences between schools are the brick, stone, and woodwork embellishments around windows and doors. Gothic Revival was the most popular schoolhouse style and was also the style predominant in houses of that era.

Life span of the schools was relatively short. Most were phased out in the 1920s when the automobile brought improvements in roads that enabled students to be transported into towns. Some, however, continued to operate as schools into the 1930s and even early 1940s. Though they were no longer used for learning, the sturdy buildings were not boarded up or forgotten. Electricity was added and many were used for another 20 years as meeting halls and polling places.

Most of the schoolhouses that have been converted to homes have been carefully remodeled to retain their original character. Despite the fact that additions have been built, porches, side doors, and back doors added, and window openings shortened to fit modern storm windows, most can still be identified as former schoolhouses. Those with bell towers retain a special charm, but most of the towers deteriorated and were removed.

A few, however, defy identification even at close range. With aluminum siding added over the brick, the only visible clue to being a schoolhouse is roof overhang scrollwork and an opening in the siding over the door to show off the nameplate.

Inside, the former schools look like any other modern, comfortable home. In some, the high ceilings have been converted into a second story or a loft overlooking the living area. The classroom portion has been divided into living room, bedroom, and kitchen areas; while coat alcoves serve as closets, utility rooms, and bathrooms.

One-room, red brick schoolhouses may have outlived their original purpose, but they still stand as monuments to our educational heritage and reminders of a much simpler, slower-paced way of life.

Rod King

First Monday

It's Monday morning
  and yet,
miraculously enough,
  no one overslept,
      missed the bus,
      forgot his lunch money.
No one spilled orange juice,
      stepped on the dog's tail,
      or even slammed the door.

On the refrigerator
  hangs this week's calendar,
its fat white squares
  filled with jottings:

      dentist appointment
      piano lesson
       aerobics
      Bible study
      drama club
       cleaners
      allergy shots
      racquetball...

But for now,
  with September sun
  shining through my
  starched priscillas,

I pour a second cup of coffee,
  watch sun rays play near freshly cut mums,
and
  lift my cup
   in a mute-salute
   to this Monday morning
so well-begun.

Mary Lou Carney

Photo Opposite
MUMS FOR MOM
Walter Chandoha

Treasures of Gold

The memories of a country school
I suddenly left behind
Are treasures I have dusted off
In the attic of my mind.

The "swimming pool" at the
    country school
Was a pond across the stile,
Where boys dared stray in early May
For nearly a country mile!

The dried leaf huts in the schoolyard
Became shelters from the rain,
Where lunch pails were brought
    with storybooks
Of Sally and Dick and Jane.

I learned to read and write, and play
Games like "Prisoner's Base" and "Tag."
I learned the patriotic songs
And true respect for the flag.

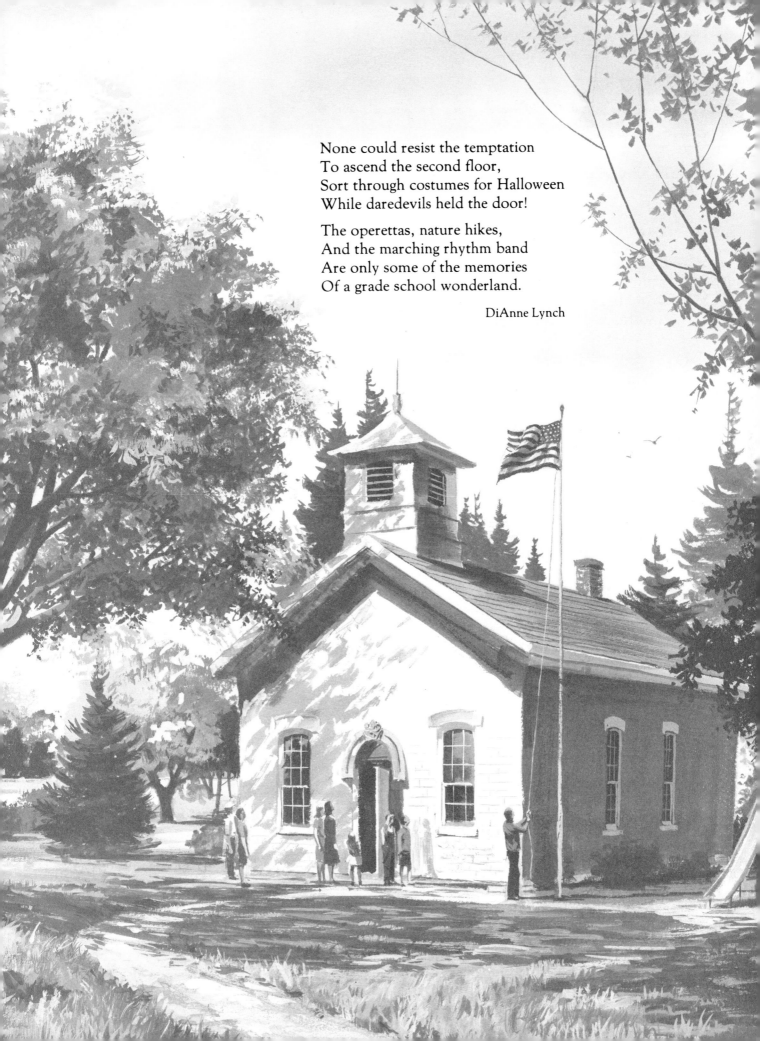

None could resist the temptation
To ascend the second floor,
Sort through costumes for Halloween
While daredevils held the door!

The operettas, nature hikes,
And the marching rhythm band
Are only some of the memories
Of a grade school wonderland.

DiAnne Lynch

First Day of School

She thought how lonely was her lot
As the school bus drew away,
And the long hours stretched before her
Of a strangely quiet day.

The house looked uninviting
As she turned to go indoors
To tackle in its silentness
A mother's waiting chores.

But then her eyes beheld someone
More lonesome yet than she,
For the children's Pal stood statue still
Beneath the old elm tree.

"At least," she thought, "I understand
Why they must board a bus.
At least I understand tonight
They'll all return to us."

But Pal, who's followed at their heels
Each hour for weeks on end,
Just knows that he's abandoned here
Without a child for friend.

"Come, Pal," she called, "you're not alone.
We'll share this day, we two,
And be right here to welcome them
When the waiting hours are through."

The dog looked up and wagged his tail;
The mother stroked his head.
And then the two walked toward the house
With both hearts comforted.

Virginia Blanck Moore

Photo Opposite
BACK TO SCHOOL
Walter Chandoha

Molders of
the Future

Most folks well worth a memory
   Have statues still in stone,
But teachers mold their monuments
   In living flesh and bone.
The student who goes out in life
   And makes a famous name,
Admits unto the heart of it all
   Some teacher shares the fame.

I never hear a pianist
   With talent true and rare,
But in the shadows I can see
   A teacher standing there.
No skillful doctor ever saved
   The lives of human kind
Without the seeds some teacher stored
   Within that fertile mind.

All lawyers, dentists, engineers,
　　All who are beloved by men,
Remember what some teacher taught
　　And quote it now and then.
No actor, writer, carpenter,
　　No boxer, you'll allow,
Pursues a chosen field unless
　　Some teacher showed him how.

Yes, teachers mold their monuments.
　　They build them year by year . . .
Not like the ancient pyramids
　　So awesome and austere,
Which time in time will wear away;
　　But spurning solemn stone,
Our teachers mold eternally
　　In living flesh and bone.

Margaret Rorke

Slippery the Sloth

"OOOOOOOOPS!"

A loud cry rang out through the forest, followed by a great crash. Slippery the sloth tumbled out of his tree again.

Sloths like to hang upside down from trees, but not Slippery. He was a one-toed sloth in a two-toed sloth family. They all had two claws on their front feet; but since Slippery had only one claw, he couldn't grip the branches tightly. That's why he kept slipping. Slippery fell so often, he wished he had a parachute.

It wasn't safe to walk under a tree with Slippery above. The spiders even made a landing net for him, but Slippery fell right through it!

Slippery decided to live on the ground. When his animal neighbors heard this, they breathed a sigh of relief. They weren't afraid of other sloths falling on top of them.

Slippery wasn't used to walking on the ground. He kept going the wrong way because sloths always move backwards when climbing on trees. The faster he walked toward something, the farther he got from it.

One day Slippery backed into a bee-hive. BUZZZ! the bees warned. They chased him through the forest. No sloth ever ran so fast in his life. Then Slippery plunged into a stream.

SPLASH!

Slippery waited. When the bees flew away, he came out, dripping wet.

Slippery decided to build a hut. It would keep him safe from bees, and he couldn't fall out of a hut!

The sloths looked down from their branches. "Hey, Slippery," they teased. "Are you crazy? Build your hut if you please, but sloths live in trees."

That night a fierce storm raged through the forest. Strong winds whipped the trees, making them shake to and fro. The sloths swayed back and forth, hanging on by their feet. Branches crashed to the ground. One by one the sloths tumbled down.

CRASH! BUMP! THUD!

Slippery didn't mind the storm at all. He was safe and snug inside his hut.

Knock! Knock! The sloths banged on his door. "Please let us in!" they cried. "We're w-w-wet and c-c-cold!"

"You made fun of me when I built the hut," Slippery replied, "and now you beg to come in. Well, hurry, before you catch a cold."

"Thank you!" the sloths cried, rushing inside.

The next day Slippery helped the sloths build huts of their own. Then he sat back and relaxed in the sun.

Howard Goldsmith

Hayride Memories

I heard the shouts of laughter
Ringing through the evening air,
And toward the frosted window
I moved my rocking chair.
The moon was shining brightly
As down the country road
I saw a wagon coming,
A wagon with a load
Of young folk, young and younger,
With spirits bright and gay.
They were singing, laughing, waving
From that wagon strewn with hay.

A note of memory echoed
Through the canyons of my mind,
And I was but a girl again,
A part of that hayride.
There was Ambrose, Jake, and Lewis,
Molly, Kate, and me;
Oh, there were many, I recall,
But names don't come as freely.
Then, too, there was the driver man,
A jovial sort was he,
Who held the reins of horses, two,
And steered with "Haw" and "Gee."

Over the dusty country roads,
Down many a rustic lane,
The horses drew the wagon
With lanterns lighting the way.
The harvest moon shone brightly...
Just as it shone the night
The hayride passed my window—
How time has taken flight!
Now tractors pull the wagons,
The horses are replaced,
But those joyous shouts of laughter
Time never can erase.

Loise Pinkerton Fritz

The Witching Hour

Giant golden pumpkin
Resting in the noonday sun,
I wonder if you're dreaming
Of a magic night of fun.

Very soon you'll wear a smile
Carved by a jackknife blade,
As you glow with candlelight
While the spooks are on parade.

You'll sit proudly in the window
To view the eerie scene,
As the gremlins dart by
Celebrating Halloween.

You will radiate with beauty
As the young and very old
Are captured in your spell,
While the witching hours unfold.

Oh, giant golden pumpkin,
When Halloween is gone
The enchantment that you weave
Will always linger on.

LaVerne P. Larson

Painting Opposite
GETTING IT READY
Frances Hook

Jack-o-Lantern

Somewhere on a field's edge
Where pumpkin vines grow thick,
We'll find a bright orange pumpkin
Exactly right to pick.

We'll take it home and scoop it out
And make the rounded eyes,
Triangle nose, and a grin so big
It could win a smile prize!

Down inside we'll put a light
To shine out in the night,
And give our friends and passersby
A lovely kind of fright.

Shining from our windowsill
Out upon the street,
A cheery jack-o-lantern grin
Makes Halloween complete.

Virginia Blanck Moore

Pumpkin faces

Once there was a jack-o-lantern
When October winds were snappy,
With a countenance so pleasant
And a smile so bright and happy.
Mother said, "It would be lovely
Just to keep that smile right here,
But a jack-o-lantern withers
If it's kept around all year."

Then she said, "I think I'll do it!"
With a twinkle in her eyes,
She made that smiling pumpkin
Into jack-o-lantern pies.
The children quickly put them
In their tummies' empty places,
And since then they've all been wearing
Happy jack-o-lantern faces!

Jane Merchant

Halloween

Owls and bats and
    hunch-backed cats,
Witches on a broom,
    Masqueraders, hit paraders,
Bright October moon . . .
    Happy faces, ghostly faces,
Faces in-between . . .

All of these are
    wrapped and tied
With one word . . .
    Halloween.

Loise Pinkerton Fritz

Photo Opposite
"TRICK-OR-TREAT"
H. Armstrong Roberts

When Halloween Takes Place

The night is filled with mystery;
The dark with spooks abounds.
The garden gate creaks in the wind;
The night is filled with sounds.

There's stealthy footsteps near the door,
A tapping at the pane.
It's time for trick or treat once more;
It's Halloween again.

An autumn moon shines in the sky
So orange and so bright;
And at the stroke of midnight,
If you're sure to look just right,

It may be that you'll see a witch
A-stride a broom in space,
But only at the witching hour
When Halloween takes place.

Mildred L. Jarrell

Halloween

The golden moon was laughing
While the goblins danced with glee.
The old witch on her broomstick
Shook her finger at me.

The black cat strutted atop the fence
While skeletons hid in the dark.
The moonbeams lit the pathway
For dancing elves in the park.

The jolly pumpkin was twinkling
While the corn stalk crunched in the breeze.
The wise old owl was hooting
In the towering hollow tree.

Once again 'tis Halloween night
And, oh, the fun in store,
For every happy girl and boy
As they dash from the door to door!

Ruth H. Underhill

As Laughter in the Soul

Autumn's bright blue weather
Holds a special kind of cheer
When the frost is on the pumpkin
And the lazy days are here;
When the trees are decorated
In their most besplendored gowns
And the hills seem consecrated
As the Sun sweeps in his rounds.

There's a little deeper meaning
To the rustling of the corn
And the way the blackbirds chatter
In the early hours of morn;
In the somber silence broken
By a screech owl's eerie cry
And the wide and trailing harrows
High across the orange sky.

In the cobwebs flinging dewy,
Sparkling sails upon the breeze;
Burning leaves and smoke a-trailing,
Silver haze above the trees;
Cider mills and fiery sunsets,
Singing brooks, and goldenrod;
And songs along the fencerow
Offering thanks again to God.

In the kitchens gay and cheery,
Where a spicy odor slips
From around the gleaming fruit jars
Like a hive where honey drips!
Oh! of all the childhood memories,
Those the sweetest to recall
Are the bright blue days of Autumn
When the leaves began to fall.

When the little creek went racing
Down around the "swimmin' hole"
And the breeze so fresh and bracing
Spilled as laughter in the soul!

G. W. Goretzke

Falling Leaves

It seems that only yesterday
The leaves were coolest green.
Today Jack Frost has come and gone,
And there is a change of scene.

Colors flame among the leaves
Of trees across the town.
Occasionally, with a gentle breeze,
A few come drifting down.

Russet hues and crimson, too,
And softest tones of gold,
Scarlet adds a splash of color;
Thus, autumn's story is told.

For a time they look like huge bouquets
And glorify the town.
Then with winter's sudden gust of wind,
They all come tumbling down.

Lucy E. Russell

Virginia Katherine Oliver

Virginia K. Oliver was born in Arlington, Georgia, and educated in Florida and Georgia. She has worked extensively with children, directing school plays and working with the children's department of her church. She was a newspaper columnist for several papers, and she organized radio and television programs dealing with her hobbies—cooking and collecting cookbooks. Her poetry has appeared in many periodicals and newspapers, including *Home Life*, *Children's*, and *Ideals*. She has published two books, *Smile Along the Way* and *The Children's Magic Corner*. *Ideals* has featured Miss Oliver's poetry for over thirty years, and we are proud to present her as our Best-Loved Poet.

September Song

The September song is played on the chords
Of winds rustling through the trees,
Creating a melody low and sweet
Of whisperings in the breeze.

There is rhythmic harmony in the leaves
That, turning yellow and brown,
Are keeping tuneful and lyrical time
As they come tumbling down.

The September song is autumn's theme song,
And all nature joins to sing,
With humming and strumming in unison
That only September can bring.

A Quiet Street

It was just a quiet little street
But as I passed that way
I thought of those who lived and loved
And worked there day by day.

From just such simple homelike streets
Where parents plan and wait
Have come leaders to make history
And stand among the great.

On just such quiet little streets
Throughout this land today
Barefoot and in boy-like fashion
Tomorrow's statesmen play.

Halloween

Witches may not be popular
And ghosts are seldom seen,
But they are surely stylish when
It's time for Halloween.

Maybe black cats are unlucky
And cheese should not be green,
But what difference does it make
At time for Halloween?

Parties where folks in weird costumes
Go darting in between
Would sure seem silly other times,
But not at Halloween.

In frolic every man's a king
And every girl a queen;
Let every care be cast aside,
Tonight is Halloween!

Keeping Watch

When school is over for the day
A puppy seems to know,
And for him the hands on the clock
Seem to be much too slow.

He keeps watch in the family yard
And makes a friendly try
To wag his tail and bark a bit
At every passerby.

Such overtures of friendliness
Help him to watch and wait
To see his own small girl or boy
Come running through the gate.

Then he will bound with joyful glee
This laughing child to greet,
And patter faithfully behind
Those welcome little feet.

I Like a Simple Life

I like a simple life . . .
Those things that day by day
Keep the whole world moving
In a special sort of way.

I like kindly neighbors
With children playing near,
And family get-togethers
With those I hold most dear.

I like quiet evenings
With friends out on the lawn;
I revel in the sunrise
And songs of birds at dawn.

I take certain pleasure
In working with the soil
And watching nature's gifts
Reward me for my toil.

I like a simple life . . .
For just such little things
Really are the greatest,
And each true pleasure brings.

Moments of Childhood

No moments in childhood will linger
Or bring more joy without measure
Than those of memories of the fair
With its unforgettable pleasure.

The wonder of the merry-go-round
With music so merry and gay,
Treats of colorful cotton candy
With peanuts and ice cream all day.

The crowd with its hustle and bustle,
The awe of each small girl and boy
Almost spellbound with the magic
Of such unbelievable joy.

Little in life is so priceless
And nothing can really compare
With the thrill of those youthful days
When the family goes to the fair!

Autumn in the High Country

When autumn comes to the high country
And the air is frosty cold,
The cone falls from the fir tree
And the aspens turn to gold.

Oaks bedecked brown, yellow, and red
With nutlike fruit the branches hold,
That wildwood creatures may be fed
When the aspens turn to gold.

'Tis God's bountiful storehouse,
A warm sight to behold,
His love for deer, squirrel, and grouse
When the aspens turn to gold.

The woodbine red climbs rock and tree,
And in her arms doth hold
The world framed in her fall beauty
When the aspens turn to gold.

We hold manmade things with awe and wonder,
The Taj Mahal and Sphinx of old,
But they fall far short come each October
When the aspens turn to gold.

That God gave us the high country
'Tis the truth if ever told,
Sneak preview of Heaven for all to see
When the aspens turn to gold.

Mary Wallace Hedric

Readers' Reflections

Autumn's Here Today

The mountain maples now are sporting
Scarlet in their hair,
And they're drawing me like lodestars.
How I wish that I were there!
How I'd love to touch the gold refined
In quaking aspen tresses
And gaze into the shadowed brooks
Which autumn now caresses.

But I'm not in the mountains,
I am near an apple tree,
And the children's swing is standing
Between the sun and me.
And insects stand suspended
As though treading autumn air,
And the morning glory chalices
Are wide and blue and fair.

And rosy, glowing snow apples
Hang guilded on the trees;
And anchored to the swing-posts
Like streamers in the breeze
Are single strands of spider's silk.
Oh, how they gleam in flashes,
Shooting forth pulsating waves
Of silver dots and dashes.

And everything spells harmony
In a tranquil atmosphere;
And every sound reverberates
A muffled kind of cheer.
And every message is a song,
A song that seems to say,
There is nothing quite like autumn,
And autumn's here today!

Mark Hart
Preston, ID

Proclamation!

When the apple butter simmers
To a rich an' spicy brown,
When there's corn roasts in the makin'
And hay-wagon trips abound.

When the frost is on the pumpkin
And the bird house is "for rent,"
Then you'll know without a doubt
That summer's up and went!

Kay Hoffman
Johnstown, PA

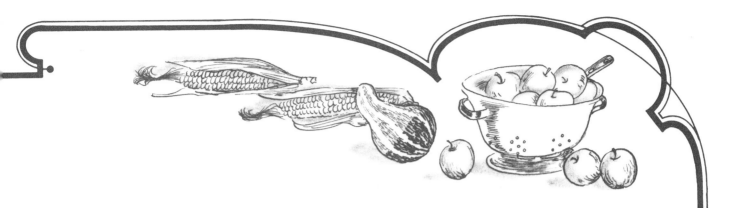

The Pumpkin Patch

With grubby little fingers,
He placed the seeds into the ground;
Patted the earth so gently,
Looked at me with eyes so brown.

"Do you really think they'll grow, Mom?"
He seemed so pleased and shy.
"With all the seeds I've planted
We'll have lots of pumpkin pies."

How those vines did flourish,
Prolific as could be,
But he's walking around that pumpkin patch
Head bowed dejectedly.

Why was he so discouraged?
There were pumpkins everywhere.
I teased him about his "orange" thumb,
But he didn't seem to care.

He said, "Oh, Mom, I'm sorry,"
Big tears swimming in his eyes.
"I grew you lots of pumpkins
But I couldn't grow you pies."

Jo Ann J. Stiefel
Apple River, IL

Early Autumn

The gypsy leaves come tumbling down
In colors amber, red, and brown.
The woodland trees stand bare and clean,
The dried sere grass no longer green.

In autumn's frosty, blue-hazed sky,
Smoke-curled wreaths of bonfires fly.
Walnuts and hickory nuts cover the ground;
Smooth, orange pumpkins in clusters abound.

Flocks of geese in V formation
Wing to a sun-warmed destination.
The full harvest moon gold-glimmers all;
Night echoes the cricket's farewell call.

Elisabeth Weaver Winstead
Nashville, TN

Editor's Note: Readers are invited to submit unpublished, original poetry, short anecdotes, and humorous reflections on life for possible publication in future *ideals*® issues. Please send copies only; manuscripts will not be returned. Writers will receive $10 for each published submission. Send materials to "Readers' Reflections," Ideals Publishing Corporation, Nelson Place at Elm Hill Pike, Nashville, Tennessee 37214.

Changing
of the Guard

The rosy, rising sun issued the order.
A raccoon fishing in a silvery stream
Washed hands and face and ambled down a footpath
Toward his den tree and a day of dreams.

A yellow moon dipped low behind a hill top,
Frogs finished serenades and closed their eyes,
An owl flew home without a feathery murmur
As dawn light brought the blue to sunny skies.

A squirrel left his nest and started grooming,
A robin found a worm and flew away
Toward a nest of hungry, growing fledglings
As roosters crowed to recognize the day.

A herd of cows stood knee-deep in the clover,
A woodchuck yawned and peered out from his den
While other daylight creatures came on duty
Until the night guard took their posts again.

Dan A. Hoover

Photo Opposite
NIGHT GUARD
Richard Wyman

Autumn Gladness

A splash of color on a hill
   Fringing a sky deep blue,
Red and yellow and burnished gold,
   Amber, green, and purple hue.
     Autumn Time!

Autumn is a flirtatious woman
   Charming all with her allure;
Flitting leaves and swaying trees,
   Vibrant with life, yet richly mature.
     Beautiful Time!

Time for square dancing, hayrides, and hikes,
   Ball games and popcorn and county fairs,
Wiener roasts, open skies, orange moonlight,
   Crisp, cool, invigorating air.
     Happy Time!

An early American room, rich warm woods,
   Baking of mince-meat, pumpkin pie,
Flickering firelight, red, braided rugs,
   Thanksgiving, homelife, family nearby.
      Cozy Time!

Taking a trip to grandmother's farm,
   Cotton pickers along the way;
Hickory nut hunting, corn in the barn,
   Smells of gingerbread and new-mown hay.
      Harvest Time!

One burst of color before she goes,
   Glowing sunsets reflect their best
Ere Nature pulls up her blanket of snow
   And lies down for a season to rest.
      Peaceful Time!
      Autumn Time!

                Lyla Moore

Country Chronicle

October is famed for its spectacular foliage display; its umbrellas of scarlet and gold span the miles from the mountains of New York and New England, down the Appalachian chain into the Blue Ridge and Great Smokies. However, October blends something more than color into its thirty-one days. More often than not, it offers a composite of all four seasons of the year.

One finds something left over from summer. For example, some days are deep in warmth, although they are short days now, far shorter than those of June and July.

There is also something of spring. Listening to the song of the bluebirds in the old apple orchard on the knoll reminds one of their enchanting liquid warble so rich and sweet in the March thaw.

The crisp cool nights with their spice of frost are the appropriate seasoning for autumn; and somewhere along the way, there is a foretaste of winter. A day of clouds frequently acts as the harbinger of the first snowflakes, adding a winter tang and touch to the hills, patching them into nature's quilt of green and brown and white.

Still, in October the main attraction is the brilliant color of the leaves and the clear blue skies overhead. It has been months, it seems, since the skies have been so clear, so blue, so high!

The vivid leaf coloring which ranges from the reds and scarlets, through the yellows and gold to the russets, browns and maroons, leaves little to the imagination. Beauty is everywhere and it is captured in the eyes of the beholder, on canvas and in poetry. It is only natural that the beauty varies from one canvas to another, or from poem to poem.

The festival repeats itself with each October, and yet it always seems new. It is one that finds new translators as the years come and go. It is one that finds the old searching for means of new expression, a new scripture appropriate to the blaze and glory of October's dazzling days.

Lansing Christman

Leaf Talk

The leaves of autumn speak to me
In fast, impatient tones
Of all the beauties to be seen
And tasks that must be done.

At other times they sing to me
In accents soft and low,
Inviting me to sit and dream,
Not hurry to and fro.

The leaves might laugh and jest a bit
And pass the time of day,
Or barely stop to speak to me
As they rush on their way.

I've talked with leaves at autumn time
Since I was just a boy,
And every year their friendship brings
A special touch of joy.

Craig Sathoff

Photo Opposite
RAINBOW OVER NORTH CONWAY, NH
Fred Sieb

November Monday

How did all the leaves
   know to fall today—

the first Monday
   of November?

In one crusty night of
   forty-degree rain,
the brittle beauty of
   October is gone.

Branches stretch empty hands
   towards skies that
      darken too early.

I drag my rusty rake
   through piles of leaves;
   mound them into mountains
      of soggy brown.

A gray squirrel chatters down at me
   from a nearby tree.
He runs round and round the trunk,
   like the endlessly moving
      strips on a barber's pole.

Then,
with a flamboyant flash
   of his furry tail,
friend squirrel scurries off
   to scavenge for winter nuts—

leaving me leaning
   on the handle of my rake,
      determining the things I should
         "store up" for coming months:
the warmth of August afternoons,
   a little July sunshine,
the gentleness of full-moon October nights,

   and the optimism
      of a March crocus.

Mary Lou Carney

ideals® Gives Thanks!

Autumn is the season of Thanksgiving, and **ideals**® celebrates the bountiful holiday in our next issue, **Thanksgiving ideals**®. Join us as we rediscover the joys of our heritage and the warmth of being home for that special Thursday in November.

ideals® also gives thanks for our wonderful readers, such as Eva Kleinlein of Jacksonville, Florida, who writes, "I have enjoyed your publication for ten years. However, I find your **Easter** issue the most outstanding."

Thanks, too, to Rebecca L. L. Horton of St. Paul, Minnesota, who writes:

When I was a child back home on my family's farm, I remember reading a specific **ideals**® story over and over, about a poor little girl in rags. Quietly, I'd cry, as I imagined myself in the drawing, poor on the outside, but rich on the inside.

Some twenty years later, I would now like to extend my thankfulness to you, to those before you, and to those beside you who recreate the ageless Spirit of our American dream on each **ideals**® page. From the depths of my childhood, I thank you.

We cherish all of our readers, and wish for all of you a blessed and happy holiday season.

ACKNOWLEDGEMENTS
FIRST MONDAY from *A MONTH OF MONDAYS* by Mary Lou Carney, copyright 1984 by Abingdon Press, used by permission; NOVEMBER MONDAY from *A MONTH OF MONDAYS* by Mary Lou Carney, copyright 1984 by Abingdon Press, used by permission; PUMPKIN FACES by Jane Merchant from *HOME LIFE*, October 1958. Copyright 1958 The Sunday School Board of the Southern Baptist Convention. All rights reserved. Used by permission. Our sincere thanks to the following whose addresses we were unable to locate: G.W. Goretzke for AS LAUGHTER IN THE SOUL; Daniel D. Rodes for IN THOSE WORK TOGETHER DAYS; Lucy F. Russell for FALLING LEAVES; the estate of Lillian Elizabeth Russell for AUTUMN'S LAST FLING.